Monthly Canvas

Vaishali Khulbe

BookLeaf Publishing
India | USA | UK

Presentation by *BookLeaf Publishing*

Web: www.bookleafpub.com

E-mail: info@bookleafpub.com

ISBN: 9789360947132

First edition 2024

*Dedicated to Eeja, my mother,
and to my mentors - Dr. Smita Mishra Ma'am
and Sujit Chakraborty sir - for guiding me to
discover my full potential and above all Thank
You God.*

PREFACE

Embark on a journey through the musings of a scrutinizing mind, traversing the different stages of a woman's life- her desires, aspirations, complaints, mistakes and perceptions. The pages are adorned with verses that capture her connection with nature, her thoughts on the world, and her struggles with the practicality of life.

The poem about a girl spreading colours is a beautiful expression of the author's vision for the world. With each colour representing different emotions, the poem highlights the need for empathy, love, acceptance, and peace. The author's words paint a picture of a world where people are kind to one another, where hatred and violence are replaced with understanding and compassion. It is a reminder that we all have the power to make the world a better place, one small action at a time.

In another poem, the author bravely confronts her own perceived inadequacies and fears of failure. Despite her struggles with academic performance, the author finds solace and validation in her passion for poetry. The poem speaks of the power of self-expression and the importance of finding joy and purpose in life.

The poem "One More Rebel" is a reflection on the challenges of navigating the real world while holding onto idealistic dreams. The author's love for teaching shines through, but she acknowledges the frustrations and limitations of the current educational system.

Overall, these poems offer a glimpse into the human experience and the various struggles, hopes, and dreams that we all share. They serve as a reminder that no matter how different we may seem, we are all connected by our common humanity.

In another poem as the world grapples with the pandemic and the loss of lives -doctors, farmers, daily wage workers and even an actor dies, the author questions the ways of the divine. There are poems which talk about her mental agony and turbulence and her accepting the fact that she is full of toxicity. But even after all this, she wants to live. These poems show how the author's perceptions change as she goes through different stages of life. That life is not a one-way thing; it comes with its own conflicts.

Through the poems "Monthly Canvas" and "Unconventionally," she paints a picture of the universal desires of women. The verses of "More than Anything" reveal the simplicity of real life, while others highlight the complexity of our thoughts. The author's words invite us to explore the conflicts we all face, each in our own way. The story of a difficult marriage, aptly named "Made in Heaven," is a reminder that institutions of societies are not meant for everyone.

But we all find solace within ourselves and in the laughter that echoes through life's journey. And we all end up being in our safe place and we end up laughing again.

Throughout the book, you will encounter various conflicts that the author deals with differently. It's a poetic exploration of the human experience and a reminder that life is full of conflicts, complexities, hopes and happiness.

Entangled Fate

She bore you.
You disfigured her.

Fed you with her nectar.
You persisted in biting her.

She toiled for your necessities.
You crushed her by asking for Luxuries.

Greener and richer, she could have been without you.
But chose to make you efficient and proper.

However you threw her out of your conscience.
Comforted yourself but bruised and destroyed her.

Ohh Mother Nature-
Her hills and oceans are not calling you.

They are asking you to stay away.
Your purgation is her destruction.

By breaking her dream of evolving together,
You have destroyed yourself altogether.

The Rainbow Girl Tale

The ribbons of rainbow –
she wore as dress.
Passing the colours,
around all the existing mess.

A butterfly got red and yellow.
A snail got the brown.
But these colours,
made some frown.

For some black and white was life.
Colours pained their eyes.
Instead of wearing the shades,
they turned to a bleach.

Tried turning everything pale again.
This is how they liked it,

Unaware of the inflicted pain.
Neglecting it, we must say.

The world was now pale.
But there still were
that rainbow girl,
The butterfly and the snail.

One hid herself.
One defended itself.
One lost some colours.
All were in pain.

The three decided to fight,
And went in three different ways.
Those colours inside,
Still spreading like blaze.

In between all this, Rainbow came and said-
The world, my kids, has failed many.
The same world, my kids, erased many.
But as long as you are here, spread the colours.

And this is how,
The snail, the girl
The butterfly
Forever stayed.

Existential Crisis

The question often arises.
Buzzing building or a peaceful lane?
Boat or the metro trail?
Framed inside the metro's window,
eyes on the boat.
And the question still arises,
Where does the heart want to go?

This is not a question of innocence or
experience,
It is rather of satisfaction.
A part of it is in the family,
the other part is not in the profession but
passion.
But the question still arises,
Buzzing building or the peaceful lane?
Boat or the metro trail?

Often we think, the world decides which way to
go.
But it is our comfort and fear which are not
letting us move.
We ourselves are responsible for the things we
do.

Will calmness meet me in the boat amidst the
river?
Or looking around, will I still be thinking of my
existence?
The question still remains the same,
Buzzing building or a peaceful lane?
Boat or the metro trail?

Ethar

Ethar was a man I loved so much.
It was not that he felt like Home,
he was my home. From being my
morning sunshine to the moonlit breeze
of night and everything in between –
He was my food, my water –
my hard-work, my relaxation –
my aid and my prescription.

But I always wanted more from Life –
more comfort and more standards.
So I stepped out from my Ethar
and started creating and earning.
And everything improved bit by bit.

As a shed was built outside our place,
now the sunshine never felt so strong.
Ethar and I set up some lights around,
which dimmed the moonlight to some extent.
I filled the house with more and more things –
slowly but steadily, the comfort kept on
increasing.

Ethar's other parts - his family and relatives
felt a little suffocated in our newly built house
so they kept on drifting away from it.
It was all okay till Ethar's Mom and Dad
started having problems. They said
I have destroyed the home and crippled them
too.
So Ewart and Ira, the parents, started moving
away too.
Some parts of Ethar were still for them,
but he still was a home for me.

But I didn't compromise
and made our life more sophisticated.
And soon there was no space for Ethar's way of
living.
So we slowly started cutting off parts of him
and the bare minimum was left of him.
Ethar was still someone who calmed my mind

and he was still my relaxing time, still a home to
me.

But now I know, I am slowly destroying him
and have rampaged many parts of him.
But what is left of him, I am trying to revive
cause he still is my Home.
But it was too late and Ethar died.

I tried my best to find a home somewhere else.
And found out, he was my only place
that always provided me with the best of
feelings and things.
Now in my House of Comfort,
I suffocated myself to death.
And you know what,
I even killed Earth's parents – Water and Air.
Ethar, Ewart and Ira, I mean to say.

Varied Vastness

Vasts are the forests
and scary too.
But once one with it,
They nurture you.

Vast are the seas,
and frightening too.
But once one with it,
It purifies you.

Vast is the sky,
And bewildering too.
But once one with it.
It will liberate you.

Opposite is the city,
Vast but Safe.
But why is everyone,
so Mundane?

Choose your Vastness
with much care.
Lost and Loss
are two different players.

Still Struggling

Q) What is the problem with this world?
A) There are various.
Q) What could be the reason for this?
A) The hidden bad around us.
Q) Hidden? Then who is controlling it all?
A) I think good always perspires to reach the
right place.
Q) Then who is actually hidden?
A) Good...ohh...good

My heart aches,
There is a plague.
Bad is taking over everything.
Good as they say just stays.
Why these moral lessons,
when everything which dwells is unfair.

Rain comes,
Weed grows,
Good flows,
Poor dies,
Rich survives.
Is this how everything is built?
God is among us and he is also struggling.
Bad above us is still ruling.

Satan is the one who planned it all.
Rich ruins,
Poor endures.
We all wait for Karma,
But whoop there they flourish.

Is it that bad will only turn good,
when good turns bad?
Make the community and kill the rats.
If it won't work,
all we will have is pain,
and more people with Satan.

Army was already red,
Doctors are getting the red too.
Farmers were starving,
Now labourers came in the line too.
Whoop, I quit says the student,
Middle class man and now an actor too.

Seems Apocalypse is for the rich to have rest.
For the down-and-out to have more struggles.

Noah has been killed,
To the boat the bad clinged.
Threw the just away,
And away they float.

Cause may be above us is not God –
Satan it is.
God is among us and he is
Still struggling.

Revelation

Though the sun has more Light,
Intrinsic cravings are still revealed more at night.
Passion lost in the triviality of mundane life,
Gets erupted with the tick-tock of silent inner strife.
When everything is dark outside
But seems lightened with the inner bright.
This is how darkness reveals you to your sight.

Unconventionally

Once touch yourself with closed eyes.
Sense thy nakedness with the touch.
Release your hair from bands and clips.
And feel them on your skin.

Fondle your face with bare hands.
You will love those bushes over thy eyes.
Those spots and eruptions will be tantalizing.

Go further and remove those clutches.
Whatever you were hiding,
let them give joy to your senses.

Electrifying goose bumps,
tender skin, loose and rough edges.
Every touch will bring you close to you.

Little or large does not matter.
Shed the shame and believe in you.

When he captures you in a portrait,
I wish he raises his brush to draw your whiskers.
And with the same brush, gives a final touch to
your errant eyebrows.
Takes the brush down, this time with more black
on it.

In their poem, when they describe sensuality,
Tell them that the touch of your lips is not the
only divine thing.
Your unruly hair, your greasy skin, that big toe
have sanctity too.
Don't these stretch marks give you hope of your
growth,
like every cloud's silver lining.

Your skin like flame has different shades.
A mark, a cut, a burn and a tan here and there.
But the warmth of your love and care is as
fierce.
Tell the world, this irregularity and uniqueness
make the world admire you unconventionally.

Monthly Canvas

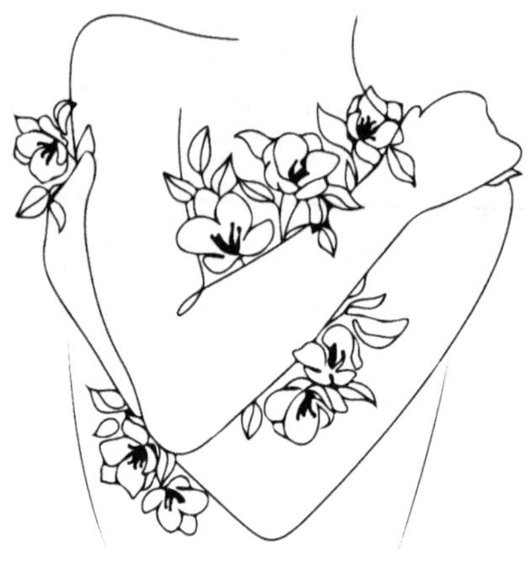

To me, it was taught that you start
your journey of being a woman when
your vagina makes your knickers its
Monthly Canvas.

But the realisation of being one, came to
me only when I had to close the two hooks
daily for others' comfort of looking at me
and had to unhook them at night for my own.

Being the only daughter,
I am the only one who got the
anatomy of my mother,
and there is a pride in it.

Cause some days, she might have looked at me
and
May be is reminded of her captive youthful
days.
And thus has given me the freedom and choice
instead of passing on the dreams.

More than periods, pregnancy and
comfort and pangs of love,
Deeds of lust can be found engraved
in every woman's heart.
If sexuality had not been a taboo but
a fact well accepted, there could have been more
stories.
More stories starting with- When I held him to
touch myself.
And not, once when he touched me.

We would have adored our bruises
and called our imperfections our uniqueness,
if beauty was a personal perspective
and not a social exhibition.

Periods and pregnancy are not what
every woman will have in her life.
Accepted or not accepted
is the fate of everyone.

And above all, womanhood is-
It is the urge of the body, not the body.
It is the urge to take care of her self
and not just the mate and the offspring.

An urge to build things, not just humans -
Things beyond our own capacities.
An urge to hold hands with equal
strength and responsibilities.

An urge to be one with the one
who has the urge to be one with our eccentricity.
But the way reality is dealt with,
I can only hope that this monthly canvas will
ever be accepted.

Ph.D. with a Cigarette

Friends gave it.
Structures and institutions made you crave for it.
Blame not the fun-filled eyes.
Reaching at the top of your ladder justifies it.

Those out of your world view-
Smell of flowers was enough for them to rejoice.
Inside your claws,
Smoke and smell both survive.

And in the bathroom,
On the roof,
who needs a friend,
I have Ph.D. with a cigarette.

Just Another Rebel

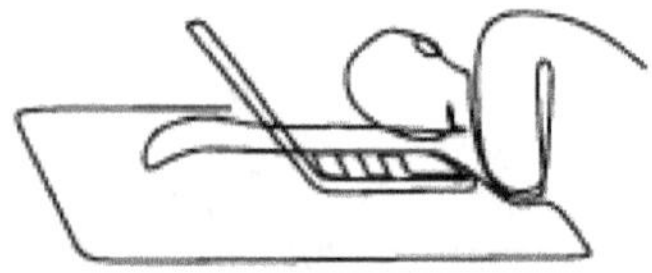

I like that you talk, but would admire you –
if you listened to others too.

Close your books and for a while look at the
reality,
Ohh I loved your answer for the originality.

I am not here to complete your syllabus,
But to add meaning to your life with it.

I want to see in your eyes a reaction,
In your mouth a perception.

Respect and discipline won't be an obligation,
But will flow freely as a celebration.

Marks are abstract, Knowledge is actual.
I am here to make you converse in a language.

To make you learn how to give words to your
thoughts.

And today, we will talk about Kazi's "The
Rebel".

Shhh...Principal ma'am is coming,
Open your textbooks and keep reading.

Love

Even without the stars,
the night was shimmering.
There is an uneasiness,
that I am trying to define through you.

Him

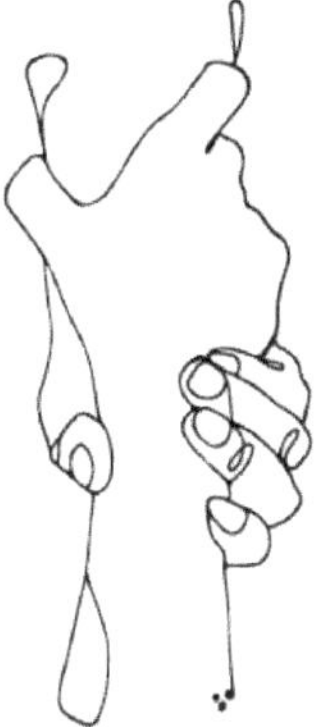

A soul that sometimes feels unstable being at
one site.
Loves the family but wants them to abide.
My emotions handled well,
while we lay in the blanket of Love-Fights.
Would understand my silence and I will
understand his.
We both will be caring for each other's needs.

But when he and I differ,
We should not repel.
Rather give each other a chance to do well.
And develop each other in all realms.
A little distance of Kms, he would not mind.
And this distance would not raise doubts in my
mind.

Till then, let me live like a reckless, eager being.
Ohhh, there is time for me to be your Queen.
A queen by attire but you will still know me as
a Mundane, lunatic and a rudimentary thing.
You tell a lot about you, while you define 'him'.
Learn to love 'you' to love 'him'.

Made In Heaven

Drop by drop, the white water dripped out of
me.
I was lying on the Earth, as if I was attached to
it.
A light came from within the Earth and pushed
me up.
Up and up and bamm... back I fell on the green.

This is when I woke up with a jerk.
Felt too empty from inside.
I wanted to hold a hand,
But there was no one by my side.

It was just a body breathing,
A pink body with dashing eyes.

Its upper trunk moving up and down.
But I, I felt nothing -

No thoughts could be transferred,
Cause it knows nothing of my language.
I tried to bring my hands close to it.
But its warmth couldn't be held.

I came close trying to take its breath inside me.
It woke up and kissed me.
My whole body shivered,
Shivered with the language of Love, I couldn't
decipher.

The kiss made me lay back,
And again I was on the Earth.
This time the Earth sucking something out of
me.
Then flowers grew on my body and butterflies
around me.

A gusty-blustery wind came and took me to the
sea.
The Sea vast and deep, as we humans don't
know of it.
And it was something, I really could fit in.
This time I had sea plants, corals and fishes
around me.

I connected, connected and connected.
And the grainy sea bed pulled me.
Pulled me and I woke up again with a gasp.
Now the body had a smile.

I touched it and turned it into glitter.
Spreading all around me and litter.
I was in each and every one of its particles.
But I couldn't still smell it on me.

I collected myself again,
And this time tried to kiss it.
My body burnt, burnt with its existence.
It, it took my fire and it screamed in pain.

Now we both lie together,
Enclosed in *frames.
We were a Match Made in Heaven,
For our *trails.

*Photo frame for the deceased
*Generations, family members

Flakes

I felt the cold,
and smiled
Realised hope is a lie.

Took the clothes off,
Fell into the snow.
Flakes pierced my soul.

I desired, at once,
to absorb all the pain.
Ended up Laughing again.

From the old Register

That day I was crying.
Crying for what I have done to myself.
It has always been tough to shoot out big lies
This time I lied cause I was losing my Life.

This boy, then a stranger,
Held the tear
and said I don't deserve this.
For me, he is all ears

A stranger judges less and cares more,
who knew this strange concept of strangers,
although for a short moment,
will make us one.

That day, I told him everything
All my fears and all my dreams.
That what I have made of myself,
in my invisible illness.

Above all I have lost my spirit
I told him of my unrealistic dreams,
of trying to be away from my screams,
I told him everything.

I have told this to nobody
Not even to me,
And at last he said
Ahhh.... That's Nothing.

He caught hold of my head
And said I have seen nothing
as beautiful as this
Wobbly head placed above my skeleton.

He says that my eyes still have light
Light of the unfulfilled dreams.
My slow breath
is stronger than my loud screams.

That day, I asked him,
if I could dance with him.
Cause I wanted to do that so badly.
Flight landed, we had our food and the close
dance too.

And for that short time
I was away from me into somebody.

Wola, the guy next to me said – Wake Up,
The flight has landed, indeed.

Away

Away is a far-off place to be.
Amidst the chaos, into the peace.
Motions cease, promotions don't please.
Range and dilemma don't exist.
Dearth of that pain in the brain,
Of that ache in the heart.
Away is a far-off place to be.

Mediocrity surrounds.
Technology freaks.
Yoga bores.
Rational or emotional –
Nobody you are.
It doesn't hurt anymore.
We don't love anymore.
Neither peaceful,
Nor revolutionary.
Go! Leave!
Away is a far-off place to be.

Toxicity

It is inside me.
It wants to tear my whole head.
Now it is not even looking for the correct outlet.

After being misunderstood so many times,
I want nobody to understand me.
I have trapped myself in someone else's words.
I have lost that free spirit.

Sitting with people,
I used to be away in my thoughts.
Now I listen to every word.
I wish not to be misunderstood anymore.
I listen to everyone who comes to me.
Finally I have stopped listening to me.

I have got no 'ifs' and 'buts'.
There are no questions.
I live and live and live,
In this living, I finally have no life.

Earlier I failed many,
This time I am failing myself.
I am tired of doing it again and again.
Finally I am weak in the knees.

A stab in the stomach right now
Will feel more like life given to me.
My inner self has become too toxic.
I finally want someone to hold me.
But right now it is just Toxicity.

Entirely Me

When in school,
my friends were discussing
the money they had spent
for coming to the event.

There were cars and autos in their talks,
when I suddenly said,
the bus takes ₹5 instead.
They all laughed.

And it took me time to understand
that they were showing wealth,
when I thought they would be proud
that I was able to spend the least on the rent.

And when they were thinking of
the fragrance of mud after the rain.
My mind had thoughts only of the smell
Of the hot dal and halwa that my mother made.

When everyone was talking about
Harry Potter and Ruskin Bond,
I am afraid that I started with
a Chetan Bhagat.

I scored less in my board
But wrote a poem for my best friend.
Although nobody cares about my school marks
now,
After 12 years, my friend has still kept the note.

I felt bad for never being a part
of the choir or the basketball team,
But I have kept my certificate
for the best handwriting.

Years later I have learnt that
I can only be happy,
When I start loving
my choices and being me.

Now I am not afraid of my collections in my
cupboard,
and also exploring Ruskin Bond at this age.

'Kehta Hai pal pal tumse' is my love song.
And I don't listen to Ed Shereen.

The late night scooty rides –
is still my favourite thing to do,
instead of eating at a fancy restaurant.
Although I do love dancing in the club.

Beautiful houses,
Clean and wide roads.
Old buildings and abandoned places,
These are my things to explore.

Unlike a few poets who said-
You are what you read
and whom you meet.
I feel No.

There is a lot
that takes birth in me.
And they are
my own dreams.

While I still read you,
It enters the periphery,
The core is,
Entirely Me.

Everyday Things

More than anything,
I miss that Snake
That appeared daily,
during my Evening Trails.

My most captured thing,
was the evening sky.
Turning red, orange and blue.
The same color, birds at dawn fly.

A cat black and white,
slept by my side,
when I shivered
at the thunder outside.

What emerges in my mind often,
is the discarded peaceful building,
covered with ever-growing vines,
silently in love with its new Greens.

Krishna Janmashtami, the date,
When a cow from somewhere,
came outside my gate.
And was offered the first roti prepared.

The kid that his mum left with me,
knowing not my whereabouts,
as she had a doctor to see.
And I was happy with my visible accountability.

Everything seemed to roam,
So freely with glee.
Cause Love is humanly.
But trust, care and respect are Heavenly.

Safe Space

Why are we even looking for a safe space?
Aren't we adult enough to be our safe space?

Even before having our safe space,
We are bringing kids into our house.

Who will give them the safe space,
when even you haven't found yours?

Your safe space can be anything-
Your art, your desire, your person.

Even your bed.
But what if it is your mind which is not set?

Your mind is cluttered,
May be degraded by few.

But pick it up, declutter it.
And start being you.

And now your safe space is no one else,
Nothing else, but you.

You will be a safe space for many now,
But let them grow, grow apart from you.
Make them their complete safe space too.
Cause remember, your safe space is only you.

Work on it from time to time,
Cause the divine is making a way through you.

Never forget – Universe's chosen
Safe space is always 'You'.

That's How The Light Gets In

You know how beautiful
It would have been to
cry, cry and then die.

Cause if someone truly understands the pain,
he would understand that
dying is much easier than crying.

To be dead is better than
waking up dead and be able
to feel the pain.

But hope is something which keeps
the little thing beat, beat and beat.
Loved ones are someone who
hold you with the love leash.

Why on Earth I got it?
To make me understand
that this world is more than
What I understand of it?

Weakness

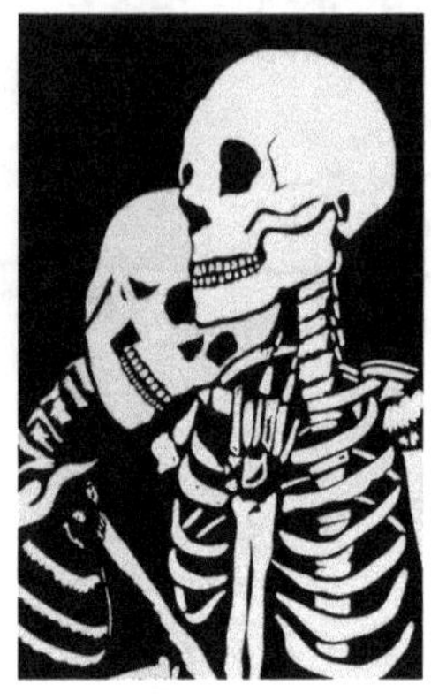

Fighting with self and fighting with the world
can be synonymous too.
Looking for sameness in other people can be
your failure to cope up with the reality blue.

Call it immaturity, say you have not grown up,
Call it self-obsession, give it any fancy name.
But the many fights ultimately
turn out to be the same.
Fighting with the self, fighting with the world
can be synonymous too.

I was expecting something from you.
I did that for you.
It was never about 'You'.
It was always about 'I'.

Your expectations,
your actions killed you.
It is not what they did to you;
it is about 'you'.

Strength is needed to be there
where you are.
It is you who lacks it,
not their devotion which needs a push.

You not getting something from people,
is not their fault, it is yours and
 will always be yours.

You still need to ask yourself,
Do you really have the strength?
Your ideas might have power but
What about your spirit!

Remember the fight is not with the world,
The fight is with you,
and both can be synonymous too.

Stuck

Once you dissolve yourself into the hustle,
these calm places will start to scare you.
A lonely hut on a mountain
will take away the peace from you.
For them to be serene,
you need to be willing
to come into the state of absorption.
Only hard things dissolve
and only soft things absorb.
Be it humans, situations, places, things –
they all come under these two categories.
We are just lost when we are stuck in between.

Nondualism

Heat in the mind, cold in the heart,
Pain and beauty aren't always apart.
Wet eyes, thirsty throat;
Pain and beauty aren't always apart.
Breathing and dying simultaneously,
Pain and beauty aren't always apart.
Lie and Laugh; Chaos and Calm;
Pain and beauty aren't always apart.
Torn and together, Stuck and Flying,
Pain and beauty aren't always apart.
Sanity of this world makes you insane,
Cause Pain and Beauty aren't always apart.

UNLOVE

You not only taught me to love,
You taught me to unlove as well.
Now I have stopped trusting myself.
The day I will forget you,
I will question my ability to love,
and its existence.

CALL OF DUTY

Let my kitchen be in shambles for a while,
First the words in my mind need an exile.

VICTORY

Barren heart stops fighting for ideal,
and starts looking for practical.
It wins the battle,
but without a victory.

NAKED

Only a naked woman
can truly see the nakedness
that lies in everyone's eyes.

UNIQUE

The way unconventional is dealt with,
I can only hope that Unique will still be a thing.